CW00600931

CRICKET
LAWS & TERMS

AXIOM PUBLISHING

ISBN 0 947338 09 8

Axiom Publishing
108 Rundle Street
Kent Town
South Australia 5067

Compiled by
Peter Scholefield

Illustrated by
Greg Willson

AXIOM PUBLISHING

CRICKET
LAWS & TERMS

CONTENTS

PREFACE

Cricket is a very peculiar game for the uninitiated. When a bowler approaches the wicket with a short leg, the spectator could be forgiven for picturing the poor man running to the wicket with a pronounced limp.

This book has been designed to aid the spectator, whether at the game or viewing on television, to understand the intricacies of the game, and to learn of the evolution of the game over the years.

Both the Laws and Terms apply equally to men's and women's cricket (unless otherwise specified), although only the masculine possessive pronoun has been used, simply for convenience and brevity. Indeed, overarm bowling is thought to have been invented by women, who had trouble bowling past their long skirts.

It is hoped *CRICKET:* Laws and Terms will provide assistance to all followers of cricket, at Test matches or their local and school grades of the game. This little book is a handy reference to the cricket fan, but primarily its intention is to be entertaining and educational.

ORIGINS OF CRICKET

As early as 1299, the accounts of Prince Edward I contained "monies for playing at Creag and other sports". Unfortunately, Edward IV banned cricket in the 1400's and penalties were suffered by those participating in the game.

Cricket was widely played in England by 1598, when the first definite evidence of the game can be seen. The "Guild Merchant Book" of that year mentions a John Denwick of Guildford aged "fyfty and nyne years" recalling "Creckett and other plaies".

Cromwell played cricket as a boy (early 17th century) and shortly after this the game changed from a children's hobby to a sport. This was no doubt due to the interest of the gentry of the day. They weren't particularly interested in the game itself, but they were vitally interested in gambling.

The first known Laws of Cricket were written in 1744. By 1770, the centre of cricket was the small Hampshire village of Hambledon. In 1772, a Hambledon Eleven defeated an All-England Twenty-Two!

The Mary-le-bone Cricket Club (MCC) was formed in 1788, and is now the governing body of English cricket. They played at Lord's established in that year. This is the home of cricket today.

Players

Each side should have eleven players, all named before the toss of the coin. One of these is to be named the captain and another is to be deputy captain. The deputy captain takes on the responsibilities of captain whenever the captain is unavailable.

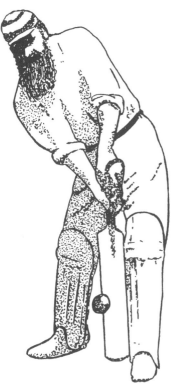

In the original Laws of cricket, the winner of the toss not only could choose whether to bat or bowl, but also the position of the pitch. This was altered in 1774, when the visiting team had the choice of innings and position of the pitch. The present rule was introduced in about 1810.

Substitutes

A substitute may field for any player who is injured or becomes ill during the match, but he is not allowed to bat, bowl or wicketkeep. The substitute may only replace a fielder who becomes injured during the match; a player who carries an injury before the match cannot be replaced unless he sustains another injury.

The first known Laws of cricket (dated 1744) stated that substitutes were not permitted under any circumstances. In 1798, the Rules were revised, now allowing a substitute who could field, but was not allowed to bat. By 1820 the substitute was not permitted to bowl, nor field at point, cover point or long stop. Another change was made in 1854; now the opposing captain could state that the substitute was not to field in a particular position. This was held in its basic state until 1980, when it changed to its present ruling.

A team usually names 12 players, one of whom is named as twelfth man, who can act as a substitute fielder. When a substitute takes a catch, the scoreboard reads:

Wasim Raja c SUB b Chappell 0

An injured batsman may also call on another player (one of the named eleven players) to act as runner if he wishes. It is preferable that the runner be a batsman who has previously been dismissed, although this naturally is not always possible. A player acting as runner must be wearing similar attire to the injured batsman. If the batsman is wearing a helmet, the runner must also wear a helmet, as well as pads and gloves.

A runner can be dismissed, run out or stumped, even if he is out of his ground and the injured batsman is in.

When the injured batsman is on strike, the runner should place himself next to the square–leg umpire. When the injured batsman is not on strike, the runner should take the position of a non–striking batsman, while the injured batsman now stands by the square–leg umpire.

The early 19th century saw the introduction of pads for batsmen. The earliest were merely wooden boards tied to the batsman's legs. By the 1850's, as overarm bowling and speed became the fashion, pads were regularly used. Older players scorned their introduction, but by this time they were deemed essential.

Helmets were introduced to cricket in the mid 1970's. Dennis Amiss was the first batsman to wear a helmet in Test cricket. Since then they have evolved from a motor bike style helmet to those we see today. As with pads, the introduction of helmets was scorned by older players, but they, too, are here to stay.

A batsman who retires through injury or illness may only resume his innings at the fall of a wicket or upon the retirement of another batsman.

The retirement of a batsman is signified in the scorebook as retired, with the reason for his retirement:

Oldfield   retired hurt   41

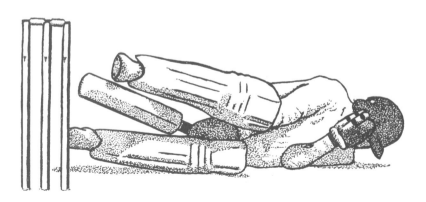

The Umpires

Two umpires should be decided upon before the game, who will act at all times with complete fairness to both teams. Any particular conditions for the game, or any changes to the rules, are to be agreed upon by both umpires and both captains before the beginning of the match.

Two umpires are decided before the game, and they act at all times with complete fairness to both teams. Any particular conditions for the game, or any changes to the rules, are to be agreed upon by both umpires and both captains before the beginning of the match.

The playing conditions should be decided only by the umpires, with regard to the weather and bad light. If the umpires decide that the light is poor, only the batting side has the option of continuing play or not. The captain of the batting side (the batsmen may deputise) may choose to continue, but if he does, the light must worsen before play can be stopped.

The umpires should also seek the approval of both captains if an unusual event causes a stoppage in play. (For example, as has happened on several occasions, crowd disturbances or riots cause play to be disrupted.)

One umpire is in control at each end (they swap ends after each team has had one innings). The umpire at the bowler's end stands behind the stumps, but not in a position where he blocks the view of the batsman, or the path of the bowler.

The other umpire stands on the leg side, level with the striker, about twenty metres from the pitch. He may move to the off-side provided he tells the fielding captain and the batsman, if this gives him a better view.

Four Runs

Six Runs

Short Run

No Ball

Bye

Wide

Leg-Bye

Dead Ball

Out

Signals of the Umpire

12

The ground should be declared unfit for play only if the bowlers, batsmen or in-fielders are endangered. Wet grass and a slippery ball are not grounds for stopping play, unless it hinders running between wickets.

Any disagreements are referred to the umpires, and if the umpires can not agree, play resumes at the stage it was before the dispute.

Early illustrations have shown two umpires were used in a match, as early as 1700. Poet William Goldwin mentions two umpires in a poem published in 1706. Umpiring has never been an easy job, and with the advent of slow motion replays, the umpires have been under minute scrutiny. For some time, there has been debate whether a third umpire with the aid of television, should operate off the field. To date, nothing has come of this.

The Ball

A new cricket ball should weigh between 155.9 grams and 163 grams (5 1/2 ounces and 5 3/4 ounces). Its circumference should be between 22.4 cm and 22.9 cm (8 13/16 inches to 9 inches). The bowling team can request a new ball (in matches longer than three days) after a stipulated period. In Test cricket this is 85 overs. However, the minimum period is 75 six-ball overs or 55 eight-ball overs.

The 1744 rules stated that a single ball was to be used throughout the match. This was changed in 1798 to allow a new ball at the beginning of each innings. In 1907, this was changed again to allow a new ball after 200 runs had been scored, but this lasted only until 1945. Since then, many permutations involving the number of overs bowled, the number of runs scored and the number of wickets taken, have been used to determine the taking of a new ball.

It is not compulsory to take a new ball when it is due, and often it is advantageous to use the older ball which usually spins more.

For women's cricket and junior cricket, the measurements may differ slightly.

Women's: Weight – 140g to 150g (4 15/16 – 5 5/16 ounces)
          Size –   21cm to 22.5cm (8 1/4″ – 8 7/8″)

Junior: Weight –   133g to 143g (4 5/16 – 5 1/16 ounces)
          Size –   20.5cm to 22cm (8 1/16″ – 8 11/16″)

A ball lost, or damaged, is replaced by one which is in a similar condition.

A cricket ball has a core of cork, which is surrounded by twine to make it round. This is covered by two hemispheres of leather (usually red), which are stitched together producing the seam.

In 1927, the circumference of the ball was reduced (from 9 — 9 1/4 inches to 8 13/16 — 9 inches). This has been the only change in the ball since the mid-1700's.

The Bat

A cricket bat must have a wooden blade. The blade is not to be wider than 10.8 cm (4 1/4 inches). From the top of the handle to the base of the blade, the bat must not be longer than 96.5 cm (38 inches). There are no weight limitations.

The development of the bat has largely mirrored the development of bowling styles. Originally a curved baseball-like bat was used. With the development of over arm bowling, the bat progressed to its present shape. There was no size limit until 1771, when a Ryegate batsman came to the pitch with a bat wider than the wicket itself!

A maximum measurement was then drawn up, and this has remained the same since.

A limitation on the length of the bat was introduced in 1835. At this time bats were made of one piece, but soon after the handle and the bat were made separately. Today the handle of a bat is made of cane, separated by several thin strips of rubber, then surrounded wholly by a rubber cover.

The Pitch and Wickets

The wickets are placed 20.12m (22 yards) apart, and the area between the wickets, and from 1.52m (5 feet) from the middle stump on either side constitutes the pitch. The wickets are 22.86 cm wide (9 inches). There are three stumps which are placed so that the ball cannot pass between them. They are 71.1 cm (28 inches) high.

The length of the pitch has remained the same since 1744, and is even thought to have been 22 yards in the 1680's. The distance is an old fashioned "chain", a measure used around 1600 to measure land. Why a "chain" was used for a cricket pitch is a complete mystery.

The origins of the "stumps" possibly comes from the very early stages of the game, when a tree stump was used for the wickets. Unfortunately, these weren't very convenient, and soon portable sheep pens were the target. At this time, the gates to sheep pens were known as wickets. In the 17th century the wickets were only a foot high, and two feet wide!

On the wickets are the bails. There are two on each set of wickets, both 11.1 cm long (4 3/8 inches) and they should not be more than 1.3 cm (1/2 inch) above the top of the stumps. The umpires can decide not to use bails if the conditions are too windy.

In 1744, there were only two stumps, and one bail. However, a third (middle) stump was added soon after, when a certain "Lumpy" Stevens bowled three consecutive deliveries straight through the wickets of John Small, without knocking off the bail! A second bail (a 16th century French word) was introduced several years later.

The wickets were introduced in 1744 as 22 inches high by 6 inches wide, but this has increased in steps in 1798, 1819, 1823 and to its present size in 1931. The rapid increase in the early 1880's was due to the invention of over-arm bowling, when naturally the ball began to bounce higher.

The measurement of the wickets may be reduced in junior cricket.

Width	–	20.32 cm (9 inches)
Height	–	68.58 cm (27 inches)
Bails	–	9.84 cm (3 7/8 inches)

In junior cricket, the distance between the wickets may be reduced to 19.2 m (21 yards).

Bowling, Popping, Return Crease

The line marked level with the wickets is 2.64m (8 feet 8 inches) long, and is called the bowling crease. The popping crease is drawn 1.22m (4 feet) from the stumps, parallel to the wickets, and extends limitlessly. The return crease is the line running parallel to the pitch from the ends of the bowling crease.

A crease of some description was used in 1744, and is so called because, even until the 1850's, it was marked by cutting hollows, or creases, out of the ground.

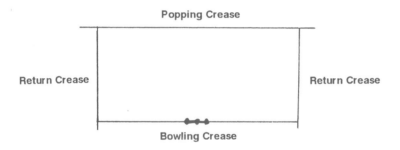

Care of Pitch

The batting captain may request the pitch be rolled at the start of an innings, or before the start of each day's play. This is the only time the pitch may be rolled, and even then, seven minutes is the maximum time a roller may be in use at any one time.

At the top level, more than one roller (of different weights) is usually available. The captain of the batting side can choose whichever roller he desires.

The pitch and outfield is mowed before the game, and before the beginning of each day's play. Watering of the pitch is strictly disallowed during a match.

Innings

The sides bat in alternate innings (unless there has been a follow-on). The captains of both teams toss to decide who has the choice of batting first, and the winner of the toss must tell the other team of his decision at least 10 minutes before the game starts.

> *The word "innings" is merely an extension of the word "in". Originally the singular "inning" was used for a batsman's time at the wicket, and the plural "innings" as the batting time of the whole team. The singular is now obsolete.*

Follow-On

A captain may enforce the follow-on if the other team fails to score the required amount of runs. In a five day match the figure is 200 short of the first team's total. In a three or four day match the figure is 150 runs, or 100 runs in a two day match. If the first day of a five day match is abandoned (e.g. due to rain) the rules are taken as if it were a four day game.

> *Before 1900, there was no option available to a captain if the opposing team did not score enough runs to avoid the follow-on. Since then it has not been compulsory, and a captain may choose to bat again. The follow-on rule originated in 1835.*

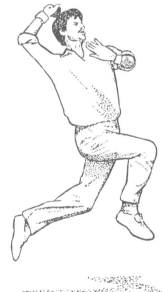

19

Declaration

An innings may be declared at any time. A team may even forfeit its second innings, as long as it tells the opposing captain and umpires.

> *Only in 1889 was a declaration law introduced in cricket. Prior to this, often the ludicrous situation arose, when a string of batsmen would deliberately smash down their wicket with their bat to bring about a quick end to an innings.*
>
> *The 1889 law permitted a declaration only on the last day of a match. In 1910 this was changed to allow a declaration after the start of the third day, and eventually the law reached its present state in 1957.*

Start of Play

After every break, the umpire calls "play". After the umpire has called, the bowler is not allowed any practice run ups, unless the umpire permits it on the grounds that no time will be wasted.

Intervals

If play is stopped (due to the finish of an innings or bad weather) ten minutes or less before lunch, the break can be taken early. The second session is then lengthened by the appropriate time. The same applies before the tea break, except the stoppage may be within 30 minutes of tea.

At the time for the tea break, if the last batsman is in, play can go for an extra thirty minutes, or until the last wicket falls.

An interval for drinks is only taken if both captains have agreed to a break before the match. There can only be one drinks break in each session, of no longer than five minutes.

Cessation of Play

The umpire should call "time" to signify the end of play before any break in the game. This includes the end of each day, the end of the match, and prior to the lunch and tea breaks. The umpires then remove the bails.

The umpires should walk at normal pace to the wickets at the end of each over. As long as he reaches his position before the stipulated time for a break, or the close of play, another over shall begin. An over is completed unless a batsman is dismissed or retires within two minutes of an interval.

A minimum of 20 overs (15 eight ball overs) are to be bowled in the last hour of the last day of a match. The last hour is taken from when the umpires signify there is one hour to go. If there are any interruptions in this last hour, the number of overs is reduced accordingly. A break of 3 minutes equals one 6-ball over, or 4 minutes equals an 8-ball over.

Scoring

The score is tallied in runs. Runs can be scored in three different ways:

1) The batsmen change ends, making their ground while the ball is in play. The number of runs scored is equal to the number of times the batsmen successfully change ends.

2) The ball reaches the boundary.

3) A penalty run is awarded.

Originally scoring was recorded by cutting marks on a stick. This practice worked well when scores were low (prior to the mid-1700's few batsmen even reached double figures), however this soon became impractical. Due to this system runs were known as "notches". At this time a small hole was cut into the ground between the stumps. To score a run, or notch, the batsman had to put the end of his bat into the hole before the wicketkeeper could put the ball there. Unfortunately this resulted in too many broken fingers on the fielder's hands.

Next the umpires held a staff, which the batsman had to touch with his bat, in order to score a run. This was still in effect in 1727, but by 1744, the rule had been changed to its present state.

The umpire should signal a short run if a batsman does not put his bat or person over the popping crease when turning for another run. Only one run is disallowed, even if both batsmen are short on the same run.

The rule concerning a "short run" has been in effect since 1774, and has been unchanged up to the present day.

If a batsman is out caught, no runs can be scored. If he is run out, only the incomplete run is not counted.

Penalties are those awarded for a lost ball, no ball, wide or illegally fielding the ball.

A run shall be scored even if the batsman takes his stance in front of the popping crease.

Boundaries

The boundary is agreed upon by the umpires and captains before the match. If possible it should be marked with a rope or line. A ball passing behind, or going under the sightscreen has reached the boundary.

The umpires and captains should agree before the start of play on the runs scored for a hit to the boundary. Customarily, a hit to the boundary scores four, and a hit over the boundary without bouncing scores six. A shot which hits the fence or boundary line has not gone over the boundary. If the ball hits the sightscreen on the full, only four runs are scored.

If a fielder has the ball in his hand, and touches the boundary, or the ground over the boundary, four runs are scored.

If the ball reaches the boundary due to an overthrow, the number of runs scored will be the runs already completed plus the runs awarded for a boundary. If the ball hits the stumps while the batsman is in his ground, overthrows may still be run.

Prior to the 1860's batsmen had to run out any hit, and boundaries were introduced mainly as protection for spectators from fielders. Four runs were given for any hit to the boundary, and six for a hit right out of the ground (it had to go over any grandstands etc.). In Australia a score of five was given for any hit over the boundary in the 1890's to 1906, when a six was introduced.

Australian captain Joe Darling (himself a renowned big hitter) pushed for a six in England at the turn of the century, but it was not introduced until 1910.

The Result

Whichever team has the most runs, after two innings, is the winner. If the fielding team, or the batsmen at the crease, leave the field without the agreement of the umpires, the umpires should award the match to the opposing team.

If each team has scored an equal number of runs, and the team batting last has finished its innings, the game is a tie.

If the match is neither won nor tied, the game is a draw.

If the winning hit is a boundary, the boundary is registered, even if this is more than the number of runs required to win.

Early cricket saw very few draws. Scores were low and innings did not last very long. The first recorded draw was in 1731; the side of Mr Chambers still needed 8 or 10 notches (runs) to reach the total of the side of the Duke of Richmond, with several players still to bat when the agreed finishing time of 7.00 p.m. came about. They hadn't completed two innings each in a full day! An unfinished game was drawn because all bets (the main reason for sport in those days) were withdrawn.

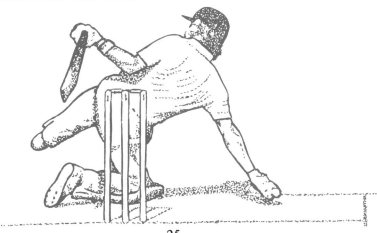

The Over

Overs are bowled from alternate ends, and may be of six or eight deliveries. The length of the over shall be decided before the match. The over is complete when the umpire calls "over". He shall do this after the final delivery of the over becomes dead, or when he considers neither the batsman or fielders regard the ball to be in play.

A no-ball, or a wide, is not counted as a delivery in the over.

A bowler can change ends as frequently as his captain likes, but he must not bowl two consecutive overs. If an over is not finished and play is interrupted, it shall be finished when play re-starts.

If a bowler becomes injured, or is suspended, in the middle of an over, any other bowler shall complete it, provided he has not bowled the previous, nor bowls the next, over.

The Laws of 1744 stated that after four balls the umpire was to call "over", so the fielders could "change over" for bowling to begin at the opposite end. The over was increased to five deliveries in 1889, as bowling tactics became more common. The six-ball over began in 1900.

Most cricketing countries have at times bowled eight ball overs, but usually these experiments only lasted a few years. However, in Australia, an eight ball over was in use from 1917 to 1979.

Dead Ball

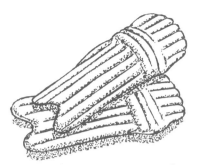

The ball is dead when: –

1. It settles in the wicket–keeper's or bowler's hands.
2. It goes for four or six.
3. A batsman is given out.
4. It becomes caught in the clothing or equipment of a batsman or umpire.
5. It gets stuck in a fielder's helmet.
6. The umpire signifies the end of the over or the end of the day's play.

The umpire declares the ball dead when: –

1. There is unfair play.
2. There is serious injury.
3. The striker is not ready and does not try to play.
4. The bowler drops the ball, or the ball is not played.
5. The bails come off the wickets before the ball is bowled.
6. Leg byes are not allowed.

The ball is not dead when: –

1. The bowler starts his run up.
2. It hits the umpire.
3. The wickets are broken.
4. An appeal has been turned down.
5. The bowler, or a running batsman, hits the wicket.
6. There is a no–ball or wide.

No Ball

The umpire should tell the batsman whether the bowler will bowl over or around the wicket, right or left handed, over arm or underarm. If the bowler doesn't tell the umpire of any change, the delivery is a no-ball. When the ball leaves the bowler's hand, his elbow must not be in the action of throwing, or it is a no-ball.

A part of the bowler's back foot must be within the return crease, and a part of his front foot must be behind the popping crease.

A no-ball incurs a penalty of one run. If runs are scored from a no-ball, the runs scored will be counted and the penalty not. A batsman can only be given out off a no-ball by being run out, hit the ball twice, handling the ball or obstructing the field.

If a batsman has been given out off a no-ball, the penalty run shall stand, and the delivery shall not be counted as one of the over.

Fair Delivery – a part of the front foot is behind the popping crease.

No Ball – no part of the front foot is behind the popping crease.

28

In 1744, the laws provided that "no-ball" should be called by the umpire if the bowler's back foot was over the bowling crease. A no-ball was dead on arrival, it could not take a wicket, nor could runs be scored. It was simply bowled again.

Between 1800 and 1810 the basis of today's rule was laid out. The batsman was able to score all he could, but could also be run out, although the penalty run was not introduced until 1829.

Only two major changes have been instituted since that date. Overarm and round-arm bowling was legalised in 1864; previously this had incurred a no-ball. In the 1960's many bowlers began dragging their back foot along the ground as they bowled, so the front foot became the centre of attention.

Wide Ball

A ball is a wide if the umpire believes it is either so high or so wide that it is out of reach of the batsman in his normal batting position. If the batsman moves to a position within reach of the ball, it is not a wide. A wide ball incurs a penalty of one run, and is not counted as one of the over. If more than one run is scored, all runs shall be scored as wides.

A batsman can only be given out off a wide hit wicket, stumped or run out.

Until 1810, wides were not deemed necessary to the game. However, in that year a William Lambert bowled a series of wide deliveries to Lord Beauclerk, to not only win the game, but also to upset the temper of his Lordship! The rule was then introduced.

From 1810 to 1827 wides were merely registered as byes, and until 1844 no extra runs (other than the penalty for the wide) could be scored from a wide.

Bye and Leg–Bye

If runs are scored when the delivery is neither wide nor a no-ball, and the ball passes the wicket without touching the batsman or his bat, they are scored as byes.

Byes weren't actually referred to in the 1744 rules. However, the first recorded score sheet of a cricket match dated 18th June, 1744, (between Kent and All England) had a record of the byes scored, and it seems that byes were registered even before this time.

If runs are scored when the ball hits the batsman, these are leg–byes. Leg–byes are disallowed if the striker does not try to hit the ball, or if the batsman does not try to avoid being struck by the ball. If this is the case, the umpire signals dead ball and the batsmen return to their original ends. A batsman can be run out, even if leg–byes are to be disallowed.

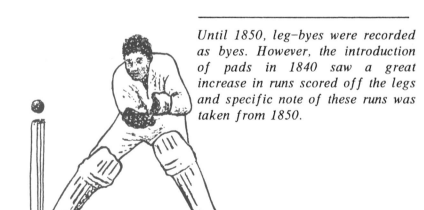

Until 1850, leg–byes were recorded as byes. However, the introduction of pads in 1840 saw a great increase in runs scored off the legs and specific note of these runs was taken from 1850.

Appeal

A batsman can not be given out, unless the fielding side appeals. An appeal can be made until the time the bowler begins his run up for his next delivery, or until the beginning of the next over in the case of the final ball of the over.

The umpire should consider all possibilities of dismissal, upon an appeal of "How's That?".

The square leg umpire can only be called on to answer an appeal in the cases of hit wicket, stumped or run out, although the umpires may confer with each other before making any decision.

The umpire's decision is final, although he may alter his decision if done promptly. The fielding captain may ask for a withdrawal of an appeal, and the umpire may cancel his decision, if the situation warrants such a move.

Even in 1744, a batsman could not be given out unless one of the fielding team were to appeal. As early as 1897, excessive appealing was considered unsportsmanlike.

Wicket is Down

The wickets are considered broken if either bail is removed from the top of the stumps. A fielder must remove the bails with the hand with which he is holding the ball.

If one bail is already off, then the other bail should be removed to break the wickets. If both bails are already off, a stump must be removed from the ground using the hand with which the ball is held.

A stump may be replaced, if all the stumps have been knocked over, so that it can be removed.

In very windy conditions, the umpires can decide not to use the bails.

The batsman must have part of his bat or person behind the popping crease to be considered in his ground.

Bowled

The batsman is out bowled if his stumps are bowled over. A delivery which is knocked on to the wickets from bat or person, and removes the bails, has bowled the batsman.

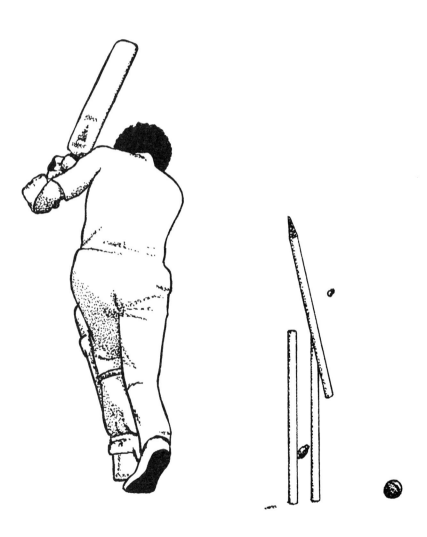

The game of cricket has evolved purely around bowling style. Batting improved as bowling techniques became more sophisticated.

Originally bowling literally meant "to bowl the ball along the ground" as in the style of lawn bowls. By 1750, however, a mixture of grubbers and fully pitched balls were seen.

The end of the 18th century saw the bowler's first major development. The "length-ball" was invented, and David Harris of Hambledon became its master. This delivery, still under-arm. would bounce only once before it reached the batsman. For the first time the batsmen were forced to use a method of defence.

The length-ball soon became outdated. In 1803, Kent player, John Willes, started bowling round arm. This caused great controversy, and new laws were made to prevent it. Thirty years later, much to the horror of the game's olders players, the bowler was permitted to raise his arm to the height of his shoulder upon delivery.

However, the round-arm days were merely a transitional stage towards the modern over-arm bowling technique. Over-arm bowling became popular, although not legal, by 1845. Eventually an unsavoury incident, when Edgar Willsher (playing for England against Surrey in 1862) repeatedly bowled over-arm despite being continually no-balled, forced the issue to be resolved.

In 1864, over-arm bowling was legalised, ending 60 years of debate. Forty years later, under-arm and round-arm bowling had disappeared from the game completely.

Timed Out

At the dismissal of a batsman, the next batsman has two minutes to get to the crease. If he deliberately takes longer, he shall be given out Timed Out. The bowler does not claim this wicket.

No batsman, in first-class cricket, has been "Timed Out". This law is a recent innovation; previously a game would be forfeited if the incoming batsman took longer than two minutes to arrive at the crease.

Caught

A batsman can be out caught if the ball hits his bat, or below the wrist of a hand holding his bat. The ball must then be caught before it touches the ground. The ball has been caught when the fieldsman has control of its subsequent disposal.

The ball must be caught within the field of play. The fielder may lean over the boundary, but must not touch or place his foot or hand over the boundary.

No runs can be scored when a batsman is out caught. However, if a fieldsman crosses the boundary whilst in possession of the ball, and the ball is in play, a score of six shall be registered.

In the early days of cricket catching was rare; obviously it was difficult to hit the ball in the air when the ball was bowled along the ground. Today's rule is basically the same as it was in 1744, although earlier than this it seems that catches behind the stumps were not given out.

Handling the Ball

A batsman can be dismissed handling the ball, if he deliberately touches the ball with a hand not holding the bat. The bowler can not claim this wicket.

> *To be out "handling the ball" is rare in cricket. Only four batsmen have been dismissed this way in Test cricket. The rule today is exactly the same as it was in 1744.*

Hit the Ball Twice

A batsman can be out "hit the ball twice" if he deliberately hits the ball after it has been stopped previously by his bat or person, unless the action is to guard his wicket. A ball struck twice when the batsman is defending his wicket cannot be scored off, unless there are overthrows.

> *Only ten batsmen have been dismissed "hit the ball twice" in all first class cricket since 1864. The present rule has been in force since 1744.*

Hit Wicket

The batsman can be given out "hit wicket" if his bat or himself breaks the wicket when he is playing a delivery, or when he begins his first run. This includes his cap or helmet.

Apart from a brief period between 1774 and 1788, when the hit wicket rule was not in force, the law has remained the same since 1744. When declarations were not permitted, batsmen often deliberately hit their wicket to end an innings.

Leg–Before–Wicket

A batsman can only be out LBW if the ball does not hit the bat before hitting his person. If the batsman does NOT try to hit the ball, and it hits the batsman in line with the stumps, or outside the line of the off stump, he can be given out LBW if the ball would have hit the stumps.

If the batsman does play a shot, the ball must have hit the batsman in line with the stumps. The ball must also have pitched in line with the stumps or outside the line of the off stump.

A batsman can not be given out if the ball pitches, or hits the batsman, outside the line of the leg stump.

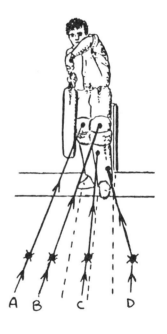

A B C D

Ball pitches on cross.

A: Out only if no shot offered
B: Out
C: Out
D: Not out

The "leg–before–wicket" (LBW) rule was introduced in 1774. At this time a batsman could only be given out if he deliberately stopped the ball with his legs, if the ball would hit the stumps. By 1788, the batsman could be given out even if the ball hit his legs accidently, and in 1823 it did not matter which part of the batsman's body the ball hit.

The rule covering the ball pitching outside off stump was introduced in 1937, and the rule covering the batsman not playing a stroke was introduced in 1970. Even in 1868, the LBW law was described as the most complex in the game, entailing great difficulties for the umpire to adjudicate.

Obstructing the Field

The striking or non–striking batsman can be given out "obstructing the field". He shall be given out if he deliberately interferes through shouting or actively interfering with the fielding side.

The game must certainly have been interesting in its earlier days. In 1744, the batsmen (striker or non–striker) was permitted to hinder a fieldsman attempting to take a catch, as long as he didn't leave his crease!

Unfortunately (for batsmen) this changed in 1788, and any deliberate hinderance on the part of the batsman to prevent a catch was illegal. Eventually in 1888, the batsman was not permitted to deliberately obstruct the fielding side at any time.

Run Out

Both the striking and non-striking batsman can be run-out. If he is out of his ground and the wickets are put down by the fielding side, he is run out. The batsman closest to the broken wicket is the one given out. If one batsman is in his ground, and the other is running towards him, the running batsman is given out.

Only the run not completed is not counted. The runs taken previously are added to the score.

Stumped

If the batsman has not begun a run, and the wicketkeeper puts the wickets down with the batsman out of his ground, he can be given out stumped. The wicketkeeper is not permitted to take the ball, unless it is hit by, or hits the batsman, until it has passed the stumps.

A batsman can be out stumped even if the wickets are broken by the ball rebounding off the wicketkeeper, or thrown by the wicketkeeper.

Batsmen have been in danger of being stumped ever since the first known laws of the game; those of 1744.

Stumpings are rarely seen today compared to earlier times. Rod Marsh, Australia's wicketkeeper in the 1970's and early 1980's, stumped only 1 in 30 of his Test victims. Australia's wicketkeeper from 1924–25 to 1938, Bert Oldfield, stumped 2 in 5 of his Test victims.

Wicketkeeper

The umpire should call "no-ball" if the wicketkeeper does not remain completely behind the stumps until the ball touches the bat or batsman, or passes the stumps.

Until the late 1700's, the wicketkeeping was performed by the bowler at his own end! Tom Seuter of Hambeldon was cricket's first specialist wicketkeeper. For nearly a hundred years, the wicketkeeper was always within stumping distance of the wickets, even to the fast bowlers. As the wicketkeeper went further back, the previously vital position of long stop became obsolete.

Fieldsmen

The ball can only be stopped by a fielder himself. He may not use any aids. If he does so, a five run penalty shall be added to the score. A ball striking a helmet left on the ground incurs a penalty of five runs.

No more than two fielders are allowed to field on the leg side, behind the popping crease. A contravention of this rule should be signified by a call of "no-ball" by the umpire.

No fielder, apart from the bowler, may encroach on or over the pitch until the ball reaches the batsman.

Unfair Play

What is, and what is not unfair play, is decided only by the umpires, who should signal "dead ball" upon its occurence.

1) The seam of the ball must not be lifted. If this occurs the umpires should replace the ball with one in a similar condition.

2) The ball may be polished by any player, however no artificial materials may be used, nor may the ball be rubbed on the ground. However, a damp ball may be dried with a cloth or towel.

3) A fielder should not deliberately get in the way of a running batsman, nor make any noise or action which may inconvenience the striking batsman.

4) Deliberate fast short—pitched bowling intended to injure the batsman shall be called intimidatory. The skills of the batsman should be taken into account by the umpire, when deciding on intimidating bowling.
A bowler shall receive one official warning from the umpire, and if intimidatory bowling continues, the bowler will be suspended from bowling for the remainder of the innings.

5) Fast, high tosses (beamers) shall be treated as fast short—pitched bowling.

6) A bowler running on the pitch after his delivery, shall receive a caution from the umpire. If he continues, a final warning shall be issued by the umpire. If this also proves ineffective, the bowler shall be suspended from bowling for the remainder of the innings.

7) Deliberate time wasting by either the batting or fielding side is considered unfair.

8) It is unfair for the batsman to steal a run during the bowler's approach to the wicket. If this is attempted, the umpire should signal "dead ball", and the batsmen return to their original ends.

   If a player performs unfairly after warnings from the umpire, or conducts himself in a way contrary to the spirit of the game, the umpires should report this to the body governing the game, who shall take whatever disciplinary action they deem appropriate.

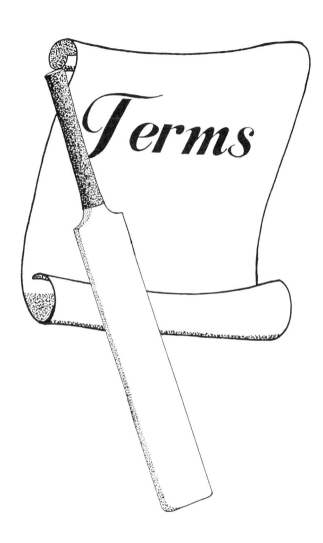

Terms

ACROSS

A delivery which goes in a straight line, but angles from the bowler's hand towards the slips. More pronounced when a right hander bowls to a left hand batsman, or a left hand bowler bowls to a right hand batsman.

To swing the bat on a different line to which the ball is coming.

ACTION

The process of bowling: bowling action.

ALL OUT

When ten of the eleven batsmen have been dismissed (or when a batsman has no one else to partner him).

ALL ROUNDER

A player equally skilled at both batting and bowling. A true all-rounder will be picked in his team on either his batting or bowling skills alone. Ian Botham of England and Imran Khan of Pakistan are true all-rounders of today.

ANALYSIS

Record of a bowler's performance. e.g. Garner 22-5-55-4 signifies that the bowler, Garner, bowled 22 overs, 5 of which were maidens. He conceded 55 runs and took 4 wickets.

AROUND THE WICKET

To bowl with the delivery arm further from the stumps than the bowler's leading arm.

ASHES

The trophy for which Australia and England compete. The Ashes are held in a small urn, which is kept at the Lord's Cricket Ground in London. An obituary was printed in *The Sporting Times* after England lost a Test in 1882, stating, "The body (of English cricket) will be cremated and the ashes taken to Australia".

ATTACK

A team's bowlers, as one unit.

ATTACKING FIELD

The fielders positioned in order to take wickets, rather than prevent runs.

AVERAGE

The average of a batsman is calculated by dividing the number of runs he scored by the number of times he was dismissed.

e.g. Colin Cowdrey batted 188 times in Test cricket, and was dismissed 173 times. He scored 7,624 runs, therefore his batting average was 44.06.

The average of a bowler is calculated by dividing the number of runs he conceded by the number of wickets he claimed.

e.g. Gary Sobers took 235 wickets and conceded 7,999 runs in his Test career. His average therefore was 34.03.

B

B

Abbreviation for bowled.
e.g. Wood b Botham 6

BACK

To play a shot with weight on the foot closest to the stumps.

A delivery which moves towards the batsman after pitching.

BACKLIFT

The preparation of a shot by raising the bat towards the wicketkeeper.

BACK UP

The movement of the non—striking batsman, preparing to run if required.

A fielder getting behind another fielder in case he misses the ball.

BAT PAD

A fielder close to the batsman, who waits for the ball to hit the edge of the bat and rebound off the batsman's pads.

BEAMER

A ball aimed at the batsman's head without bouncing. It is considered unfair.

BITE

To spin sharply upon pitching. It is more prominent on a damp or well-grassed pitch.

BLOCK

Take block: take guard to ascertain the correct position for taking stance.

A defensive shot.

BLOCKHOLE
The spot, on the popping crease, where the batsman rests his bat when taking strike.

BOARD – Scoreboard.

BODYLINE
Bowling short–pitched deliveries aimed at the batsman. It was made famous by the English team which toured Australia in 1932–33. It was designed by captain Douglas Jardine, and implemented by Harold Larwood, to contain Don Bradman. It caused great controversy and even trade embargoes between the countries were rumoured. England won the series convincingly, but "bodyline bowling" was ruled unfair the next year.

BOTTOM HAND
The lower of the hands when holding the bat. A batsman mainly using the bottom hand plays most of his shots with a horizontal bat.

BOUNCER
A delivery pitched so that passes the batsman at chest height or above. The bowling of too many bouncers is considered unfair, if it is aimed to injure the batsman.

BREAK
Spin. A ball which spins from the off–side to the leg–side is an off–break, and one which spins the other way is a leg–break.

BUMP BALL
A ball which is hit straight into the ground, and then is caught by a fieldsman, to appear as a catch.

BUMPER – Bouncer

BUY A WICKET
A tactical attempt to take a wicket, even if runs may be scored easily due to these tactics.

C

C

Abbreviation for caught. Usually followed by the catcher's name, and the name of the bowler who was bowling at the time.

e.g. Gavaskar c. Bari b. Sikander 31

C and B

Used to signify a bowler taking a catch from his own bowling.

e.g. Flowers c. and b. Spofforth 0

CARRY A BAT

To be not out at the end of an innings. Usually associated with opening batsmen. Originated when a team would only have two bats, and a dismissed batsman would leave his bat at the wicket for the next batsman.

CAUGHT BEHIND

A catch taken by the wicketkeeper.

CENTURY

A score by a batsman of over 100.

CHANCE

To offer the possibility of a catch.

CHANGE BOWLER

A bowler, mainly used to prevent scoring, who bowls to give the main bowlers a rest.

CHANGE ENDS

To bowl from the other end of the pitch.

CLEAN BOWL

To be bowled without the ball first hitting bat or body.

CLOSE/CLOSE OF PLAY
Stumps, the end of play for the day.

CROSS BAT
To play a shot with a horizontal bat.

CRUMBLE
A pitch which is beginning to break up on the surface is said to crumble.

D

DANGER AREA
The area on the pitch four feet from the popping crease, and one foot either side of the middle stump. A bowler must be careful not to tread in this area after bowling, for it can severely damage the pitch and give bowlers an unfair advantage.

DEAD BAT
A defensive shot played with little or no backlift.

DEFENCE
A shot with no attempt to score runs, merely intent on not getting out.

Forward defence – a defensive shot played on the front foot.
Back defence – a defensive shot played on the back foot.

DEFENSIVE FIELD
Fielders positioned merely to stop runs being scored, with no or little attempt to get the batsman out.

DELIVER – To bowl the ball.

DELIVERY – A single ball.

DIG IN
To deliver the ball pitched short, so it bounces high at the batsman.

DIG OUT
To hit a delivery pitched on the popping crease (a yorker).

DISMISS
To get out (either a batsman or a team).

DOT BALL
A ball from which there is no run, nor a wicket is taken.

DOUBLE CENTURY
A score of 200 or more by a batsman.

DOUBLE FIGURES
A score of ten runs or more.

DRAG

To hit the ball onto the stumps, from outside the off-stump.

To slide the back foot along the ground in the delivery action.

DROP – To miss a catch.

DUCK

To be out for zero. The term has it's origins from the similarity between the number zero and the shape of a duck's egg, which is the original term. The term was first seen in 1863, when low scoring became less common.

E

ECONOMICAL – Conceding few runs.

EDGE

To hit the ball on the sides of the bat, rather than the middle of the blade.

END

Bowler's end: the area from which the bowler bowls.
Striker's end: the area from which the batsman plays.

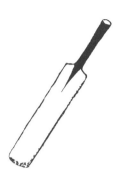

EXPENSIVE – Conceding many runs.

EXPRESS – Very fast.

EXTRAS

Those runs scored not by the batsman. i.e. byes, leg–byes, wides and no–balls; also known as sundries.

FACE
To receive the bowling.
The front of the blade of the bat (e.g. full face of the bat).

FALL – A dismissal; a wicket has fallen.

FARM
To keep the strike, to save a poor batsman from facing.

FIELD
The oval
To collect a ball after it has been hit.

FIGURES – Bowling analysis.

FIRST CHANGE BOWLER
The bowler who bowls after the first two bowlers.

FOLLOW THROUGH
To swing the bat after hitting the ball.
The completion of a bowler's action, after the release of the ball, and his consequent paces as he slows down.

FOOT WORK
The movement of the feet when playing a shot.

FORCING SHOT
A shot played off the back foot, trying to hit the ball between cover and mid-wicket.

FORWARD
To play a shot with weight on the foot further from the stumps. Forward play only developed in the late 1700's as the "length ball" was perfected.

FRONT FOOT
The foot further from the stumps.
On the Front Foot – playing forward.

FULL – A ball pitched near or past the batsman.

FULL TOSS
A delivery reaching the batsman without bouncing. Also known as full pitch, it is easy to hit for runs.

G

GARDENING
To tap the wicket with the end of the bat, in order to smooth any bumps on the surface.

GATE
The small gap between the batsman's pad and his bat, not desirable, but often seen when a batsman plays on the front foot.

GET AWAY – To hit the ball past the fielders.

GRASS – To drop a catch.

GREEN
A green pitch has a covering of grass, and is conducive to seam bowling.

GROUND – The oval (e.g. Melbourne Cricket Ground).

GROUND HIS BAT
To run the bat along the surface when completing a run.

GUARD
A mark on the ground, made by the batsman, so he can ascertain his position in regard to the stumps. Guard is given by the umpire.

H&I

HALF–CENTURY
A score higher than 50, but less than 99.

HALF–VOLLEY
A delivery pitched just before the popping crease.

HAT TRICK
The taking of three wickets in three consecutive deliveries.

HOLE OUT – To hit a catch to a fielder in the outfield.

HOWZAT – Bowler's scream of appeal to the umpire.

I.C.C.
International Cricket Conference. The governing body of cricket.

IN – The batsman, or team, who is batting.

INFIELD – Fielding area close to the batsman.

INNINGS DEFEAT
To lose a game without the opposing team having to bat twice.

INSIDE EDGE
The edge of the bat closest to the batsman, when the bat is vertical.

KEEP – Perform the tasks of the wicket–keeper.

KING PAIR
To be dismissed in each innings, off the first ball faced.

KNOCK – Innings.

L

LBW
Denotes out leg–before–wicket.
e.g. Richards LBW b. Hadlee 23.

LEADING EDGE
The edge of the bat nearest to the bowler, especially noticeable when the batsman attempts to drive to the leg–side.

LEATHER – The ball.

LEAVE
A delivery which moves away from the batsman, to the off–side, either as it pitches, or through the air.

LEG
The side of the field behind the batsman's legs. Also known as "on".
Around One's Legs: to be bowled when the ball goes behind the batsman's legs.
Off One's Legs: to hit a delivery directed at the batsman's legs.

LEG THEORY
To bowl at the batsman's body, with many fielders on the leg side close to the bat. Especially prominent in the famous Bodyline series of 1932–33, when Harold Larwood of England employed it successfully.

LENGTH

The point where a delivery pitches, in relation to distance from the bowler.

Good Length – A ball which pitches to hit the very top of the stumps. It is awkward to play, being too short to play forward, but too full to play back.

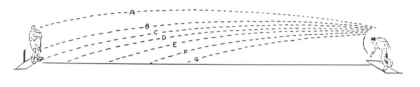

A: Beamer	D: Half-Volley	G: Bouncer
B: Full Toss	E: Good Length	
C: Yorker	F: Short-Pitched	

LIFE/LIVELY

A pitch has life, or is lively, when it provides assistance to pace bowling.

LIFT – Sharp bounce off the pitch.

LIGHT

Offered the light – if conditions become dim, the umpires may ask the batsmen if they wish to continue.

LINE

The direction which a delivery takes from the bowler's hand.

LINE AND LENGTH

The line of the ball, and the length of the ball are the basics of bowling.

LOFTED SHOT – A hit in the air.

LOLLY – A simple catch.

LONG HANDLE – Attacking shots.

LONG HOP
A ball pitched half way down the pitch, that bounces at a comfortable height to the batsman, and is easily hit to any part of the ground.

LOOSE – Poor bowling.

LOWER ORDER
The batsmen who come in last, usually bowlers who aren't expected to score many runs. Also known as the tail.

MAIDEN OVER

An over from which no runs are scored, nor are there no-balls or wides. The term comes from an old English meaning of the word: unproductive.

MARK

The beginning of the bowler's run-up.
Off the mark — to score the first runs of a batsman's innings.

MIDDLE STUMP — The central of the three stumps.

MIDDLE ORDER

The batsmen after the openers, but before the tail.

MISCUE

To hit a shot incorrectly, the ball not going where it was intended to go.

MOVEMENT

Sideways deviation of the ball from its original line. There can be movement through the air, off the pitch or off the seam.

NETS — Practice pitches.

NIGHTWATCHMAN

A lower order batsman, who goes in if a dismissal occurs late in the day, in the hope he can bat until stumps.

NON-STRIKER

The batsman who is not facing the bowling.

NOT OUT

A batsman who has not been dismissed. Usually denoted by an asterisk next to the batsman's score.

O

OFF
The side of the field on which the batsman does not stand when he faces the bowling. This term has it's origins from old horse and carriage days. The driver would walk (or the rider mount) on the near side of the carriage, compared to the off side of the carriage.

OFFER
Usually used in the negative. A batsman can be out LBW, even if the ball pitches outside off stump, if he does not offer a shot.

OLD ENEMY
In Australia, the old enemy is England; in England the old enemy is Australia.

ON
Also known as leg.
Bring a bowler on – to begin bowling with a new bowler.

ON THE UP
To hit a ball which has pitched on a good length, with a vertical bat.

ONE-DAY CRICKET
The game played with a set number of overs per innings (only one innings per team). Also known as Limited Overs Cricket.

OPEN
To be one of the batsmen who begins the innings.
To be one of the bowlers who begins bowling in an innings.

ORDER

The list of a team's batsmen. Divided into the openers, middle order and tail-enders.

ORTHODOX

To bowl spin bowling according to the coaching manual.

OUT-CRICKET

The skills of fielding, especially in the outfield.

OUTFIELD – The areas of the oval near the boundary.

OUTSIDE EDGE

The edge of a vertical bat not closest to the batsman. An outside edge often gives a catch to the slips fielders.

OVER RATE

The number of overs bowled in an hour or a day.

OVER THE WICKET

To bowl with the delivery arm closer to the stumps, compared to the bowler's leading arm.

OVER-THROWS

Runs taken when the ball is returned from the fielder poorly, and it goes past the wickets, giving the batsmen time to take another run or runs.

P&Q

PACE
The speed of a delivery. Usually associated with fast bowlers.

PACEMAN – Fast bowler.

PAD UP
To thrust the legs at the ball, rather than hit it with the bat. This makes the batsman susceptible to LBW, as he is not offering a shot.

PAIR
To be out for zero in both innings of a match.
On a Pair – to have been out for zero in the first innings of a match, and consequently in danger of achieving a pair.

PARTNERSHIP
The number of runs two batsmen score together, until one of them is dismissed.

PICK
A batsman capable of distinguishing a particular kind of delivery from a bowler is said to have "picked it".

PLACE – To hit the ball between fielders.

PLAY
To participate in the game.
To perform a shot.

PLAY AND MISS – Unsuccessfully attempt to hit the ball.

PLAY ON
To hit the ball on to the stumps. Registered as out - bowled.

PLUMB – Unquestionably
out LBW.

PUSH – An innocuous
defensive shot.

PUSH THROUGH
To bowl a little faster, usually by a spin bowler.

PUT DOWN – Drop a
catch.

PUT IN
To order the opposing team to bat, after winning the toss.

PUT ON – To score runs
in a partnership.

QUICK/QUICKIE – Fast
bowler.

R

RABBIT – A batsman with little or no batting skill.

READ
To gauge the line, length and movement of a delivery.

REPLY – The second innings score of a match.

RETURN
To throw the ball back to the stumps, after fielding.

RETURN CATCH – A "caught and bowled."

ROUGH
The footmark of the bowler on the pitch, which becomes scuffed from constant wear. A spin bowler can produce extra turn if the ball pitches here.

RUNNER – Player permitted to run for an injured batsman.

RUN RATE
The number of runs scored in a given time. An individual batsman's run rate is usually measured per 100 balls, and a team's run rate is usually measured per over.

RUN UP – The bowler's approach.

S

SAVE – To prevent runs.

SCORE-BOARD
Instrument used to show spectators and players the present score.

SCORECARD – Sheet on which the score is recorded.

SEAM
The narrow, slightly raised line on the ball, where the two halves of leather are stitched together.
To bowl trying to land the ball on the seam, for movement into or away from the batsman.

SEND BACK
To order a batting partner back to his crease, after beginning a run.

SET – To have played oneself in.

SHARP
A catch which comes quickly to the fielder.
A delivery which spins surprisingly far and quickly.

SHINE
The polish of the ball. Assists fast and swing bowling when maintained, and assists spin bowling when not preserved.

SHOOTER
A delivery which unexpectedly stays low as it passes the batsman.

SHORT
A delivery pitched closer to the bowler, so it bounces higher.

SHORT OF A LENGTH
A delivery pitched so it bounces just over the top of the stumps.

SHOULDER – The top of the blade of the bat.

SHUFFLE ACROSS
To move across the crease, before the ball has been bowled.

SHUTTERS
To bat defensively, usually looking to stave off defeat.

SIGHTBOARD/SIGHTSCREEN
Large device placed on or just behind the boundary, behind the bowler's arm. Assists the batsman to see the ball. Usually white, but in night cricket (when a white ball is used) it is black.

SINGLE – One run scored by the batsman.

SITTER – An easy catch.

SKY – To hit the ball high, usually off the edge of the bat.

SLANT – To angle the ball across the batsman.

SLOG
To swing the bat indiscriminately, trying to hit the ball as far as possible. Often seen late in a limited overs innings.

SMOTHER THE SPIN

To put one's front foot near to where the ball bounces, and hit the ball before any spin has time to deviate effectively.

SNICK

An edge which makes very slight contact with the ball.

SPELL

The length of time, or number of overs, a bowler bowls successively from one end.

SQUARE–LEG UMPIRE

The umpire stationed at the striker's end, who stands at square leg.

ST

Used to signify a batsman is out stumped, followed by the name of the wicket–keeper.

e.g. Wood st Bairstow   b. Emburey 112

STANCE

The position in which the batsman stands as he faces the bowling.

STAND – A partnership.

STAND UP

When the wicket–keeper is within touching distance of the stumps, as the bowler delivers the ball.

STEER

To direct the ball off the face of the bat, rather than hit it.

STICKY WICKET

A damp pitch which begins to dry out. A spin bowler can turn the ball very sharply off such a wicket. Rarely seen today, because of modern pitch covers which prevent water getting on to the pitch.

STOCK BALL
A bowler's normal delivery, rather than one produced occasionally.

STOCK BOWLER
A bowler who concentrates on containment rather than taking wickets.

STRAIGHT BAT
To play with the bat exactly perpendicular to the ground.

STRIKE – The batsman facing the bowling is on strike.

STRIKE BOWLER
An attacking bowler expected to take wickets.

STRIKE RATE
Batting: the run rate.
Bowling: how many wickets taken in a set period. Often measured per 100 balls; also per over or per match.

STROKE
To hit the ball, usually with good timing rather than force.

STUMPS – The end of the day's play.

SUB
Denotes a catch taken by a substitute fielder.
e.g. Laird c. sub. b. Garner 75.

SUNDRIES – Extras.

SWEEPER
Modern term for a fielder on the boundary to defend a large area of the outfield.

T

TAIL
The collective batsmen late in the batting order.

TAILENDER – A batsman in the tail.

TEST
A game played over 5 days between two sides representing countries who are full members of the International Cricket Conference. The first Test was played in 1877 (between Australia and England), although the term itself was not commonly used for another decade.

THICK EDGE
A hit off the edge of the bat which makes reasonable contact with the ball. Compare to snick.

THROW – An illegal delivery, bowled with a bent elbow.

THROW OUT
To hit the stumps directly from the fielder's return, to effect a run–out.

THROW THE BAT
To indiscriminately slog. Often seen in one-day cricket.

TON – A century.

TOP EDGE
The upper edge of the bat, when a shot is played with a horizontal bat.

TOP SCORE – The highest score of an innings.

TURN
Movement of the ball upon pitching by a slow bowler; spin.

TURN BLIND
To begin another run without looking to see if the ball has yet been fielded.

TWELFTH MAN
The reserve player, who acts as substitute fielder if required, and performs tasks, such as taking out drinks, for the actual players.

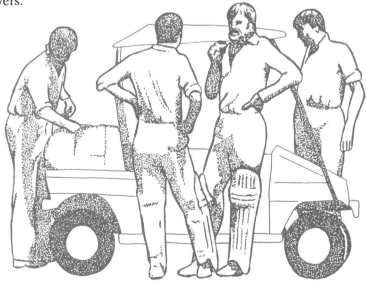

U&V

UNBEATEN – To be not out.

UPPISH
To hit the ball so it travels above the ground for a distance at a height at which it could be caught.

USEFUL
Reasonable, but not exceptional. Usually associated with a batsman or bowler.

V – The area on the field between cover and mid–wicket.

W,X,Y&Z

WALK
To leave the crease after being dismissed, before the umpire gives a batsman out.

WHIPPING – To bowl with a sudden and rapid bowling action.

WICKETS
To win by "X" wickets: to win with "X" number of batsmen to be dismissed to end the innings.
A partnership. i.e. ninth wicket = ninth partnership.

WICKET MAIDEN
An over in which there are no runs debited against the bowler, and he also takes a wicket.

WORK
To hit forcefully, usually to the outfield but not to the boundary.

WORKHORSE – A stock bowler.

WRISTY
To hit the ball with much movement of the wrists.
To bowl the ball with much movement of the wrists.

YORKER
A delivery which pitches on the popping crease. It originated from Yorkshire. It was also known as a tice, because the batsman would be "enticed" to drive when the ball was too full to be a half volley and too short to be a full toss, but this term is no longer used.

BATTING SHOTS

FORWARD DEFENCE

A shot intended merely to stop the ball hitting the wickets. Played to a delivery well pitched up, with the front foot advanced down the pitch. It is important that the bat is close to the pad, and there is no "gate" for the ball to get through.

A correct forward defensive shot. The front foot is well forward and there is no "gate" for the ball to pass through.

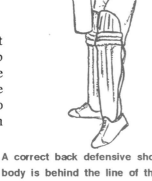

BACK DEFENCE

Shot played to a straight, short pitched delivery, in order to stop the ball hitting the stumps or the batsman's body. Care must be taken to hit the ball straight into the ground and not offer a catch to a close fielder.

A correct back defensive shot. The body is behind the line of the ball, and there is no "gate" between bat and pad.

DRIVE

An attacking shot played to a delivery which pitches just short of the batsman, or a full toss. The bat is swung in a large arc, and the bat should be perpendicular to the ground when it comes into contact with the ball.

FRENCH CUT

An attempted drive, but the batsman only hits the ball with the inside edge of the bat. A true French Cut sees the ball passing between the batsman's legs and the stumps. Also known as a Chinese Cut.

LEG GLANCE

A deflection to fine leg, played with a vertical bat.

GLIDE

To steer the ball to the third man area. Not played with any force.

CUT SHOT

An attacking shot to a short-pitched delivery aimed outside the off-stump. It is played with a horizontal bat, and the ball should go between the third man and cover positions.

PULL SHOT

An attacking shot played with a horizontal bat to a delivery pitched short on or outside the leg stump. The batsman brings his bat around his body, pivots on his feet, and hits the ball between the square leg and mid-wicket positions.

HOOK SHOT

Similar to a Pull Shot, but the ball is hit behind the square leg position. Usually played to a ball which comes to the batsman at about head height.

SWEEP SHOT

A shot played, usually to a slow bowler, with the front knee on the ground. The shot is played with a horizontal bat, and hit between the mid-wicket and fine leg areas.

BOWLING

PACE BOWLING
To bowl as fast as possible, not attempting movement off the pitch or through the air. Only the most highly skilled pace bowler can achieve movement while bowling at his fastest. Pace bowlers are also known as Fast Bowlers, Express Bowlers or Quickies.

MEDIUM PACED BOWLING
To bowl achieving movement off the pitch or through the air, at the expense of a little speed.

SEAM BOWLING
To bowl attempting to land the ball on the raised seam, so it will deviate into or away from the batsman.

CUT
Lateral movement of a delivery as it pitches. Bowled by a fast or medium paced bowler, as a fast spin bowl. A ball cutting into the batsman is an off-cutter, a ball cutting away from the batsman (one of the most difficult deliveries to bowl) is a leg-cutter.

Leg Cut Grip

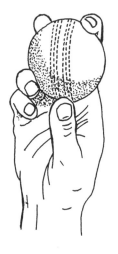 

Inswing Grip   Outswing Grip

SWING

Movement, into or away from the batsman, of the ball as it travels through the air. Swing is thought to have been introduced to cricket by J.B. King, who played for the American Cricket Team around 1897. He was also a baseball player and probably borrowed from the pitcher's curve ball repertoire.

What actually causes the ball to swing is a matter of great debate, and even a scientific paper has been produced on the subject. The paper defied common belief to say that humidity in the air was not a major factor. Instead there are a number of factors responsible. They are the angle at which the seam is held, the pace of the delivery and the number of revolutions the ball takes before it reaches the batsman.

SPIN BOWLING has been a component of cricket since it's earliest days. In the underarm bowling days, spin from leg to off was only seen until 1780, when a Hambledon player, named Lamborn, confused all batsmen by learning to spin the ball the opposite way! At this time spin was known as twist, and a spin bowler was called a twister.

FLIGHT
To deliver the ball with a high trajectory, in the hope that any breeze present will effect the line and length of the pitching of the ball.

FINGER SPIN
To spin the ball using the fingers, as compared to the wrist spinner who uses his wrist.

ARM-BALL
A finger spinner's variation. A delivery which does not deviate.

OFF-BREAK
A delivery which spins from off to leg. Usually related to a finger spinner.

WRIST SPIN
To turn the wrist at the moment of delivery, causing the ball to deviate as it pitches.

LEG BREAK
A delivery which spins from leg to off. Usually associated with wrist spinners.

LEGGIE – (Australian term) bowler of leg breaks.

WRONG-UN
A wrist spinner's delivery which spins the opposite direction to his normal bowl.

GOOGLY

A delivery from a right-handed leg spinner which spins as an off spinner. The righthander's wrong-un: This delivery, invented by Bernie Bosanquet of England around 1900, made the batsman "goggle" at the bounce, hence it's unusual name.

BOSEY

An Australian term for a googly, named after it's inventor.

CHINAMAN

A Chinaman can be two different things, depending on where you are. In England, a left arm wrist spinner bowls a Chinaman when the ball spins from off to leg – his normal delivery. However, if you are in Australia a Chinaman (still bowled by a left arm wrist spinner) spins the opposite way! In other words, it is his wrong-un.

TOP SPIN

A delivery from a wrist spinner which does not deviate as it pitches, but gains pace.

FLIPPER

Similar to a top-spinner, but usually bounces a little lower than a regular delivery.

FIELDING POSITIONS

A fielder is permitted to be placed anywhere on the field, as long as he isn't on the pitch itself. However, it must be remembered that no more than two fielders are allowed behind square, on the leg side.

The two diagrams below show the set positions on the field and the slight variations which can be made in any area of the field. When these are combined, all the possible fielding positions have a descriptive name, as can be seen in the large diagram overleaf.

The positions in these diagrams assume the batsman is right-handed; for a left-handed batsman, the positions are mirrored.

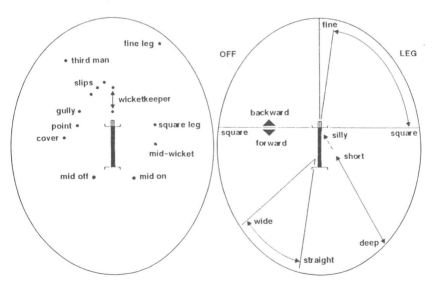

REGULAR FIELD POSITIONS

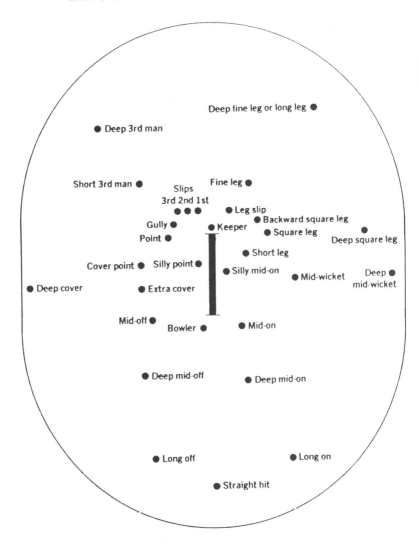

COVER

The position where the most athletic fielder is usually placed. It was originally known as "the man who covers the point and middle wicket".

FINE LEG

Often used as a synonym for deep fine leg. The true fine leg position is rarely seen in cricket today; even only 50 years ago the area was always known as long leg.

FLY SLIP

So called because a fielder is stationed there to catch an edged shot which "flies" over the heads of the slips fielders.

GULLY

So called because it is the channel, or gully, between the slips fielders and point. It only became a regular position at the turn of the century, and nowadays most teams have a fielder who specializes in this position.

LONG STOP

The position behind the wicketkeeper who fields the ball if the 'keeper misses. Nowadays a long stop is not required, but in the days before specialist wicketkeepers and protective equipment, the long stop was a necessity.

MID OFF/MID ON .

Originally these two positions were known together as "middle wicket". This soon became confusing, and the distinction was made: middle wicket off and middle wicket on. The modern terms are merely contractions of these phrases.

MID WICKET

This position is extremely adaptable and can be short, wide, square, or silly. This is a modern phrase dating from around 1930.

POINT

So called, because the point fieldsman in older days fielded within reach of a batsman's pointed bat. At times, the position was even called "bat's end". Over the years, point moved further and further from the bat.

SILLY

Any fielding position very close to the batsman, named because a fielder must indeed be very silly to stand there. These positions were regularly used as early as 1878 when Harry Boyle of Australia specialized in the silly mid-on position. With the advent of helmets, fielders have become "sillier" and "sillier".

SLIPS

A captain may place as many fielders as he likes in the slips, but usually four is the maximum number. The number of slips will be reduced as a batsman's score increases or the ball becomes older. The slip is placed to catch any edged shot from the batsman. The slip is so called because an edged shot is usually the result of a batsman's mistake or "slip".

SQUARE LEG

One of the oldest fielding positions, which has been in its current place since around 1800.

THIRD MAN

Like the position of point, the third man originally was very close to the bat. In fact, complaints were made in the 1850's, when a Rev. Canon McCormick fielded so close at third man, he could catch the ball as the batsman blocked! As slips became more popular in the 1890's, the third man moved deeper to its present position.

INDEX

CRICKET NOTES

CRICKET NOTES

Also in this series:
Cricket Trivia Declared

AXIOM PUBLISHING

**108 Rundle Street,
Kent Town,
South Australia.**